On July 14, 1789, the Bastille — the ancient fortress-prison, hated because it symbolized despotic rule — was besieged and taken by the citizens of Paris. This was the climax to one phase of a national insurrection, and it marked the beginning of another. Eventually, feudal power would end and a new pattern of society would be born in France. As an observer commented, the event would contribute to the happiness and prosperity of millions of descendants, and had taken place "with but few days' interruption to the common business of the place."

PRINCIPALS

LOUIS XVI, king of France.

MARIE ANTOINETTE, the queen.

DUC D'ORLÉANS, head of a branch of the royal family which traditionally opposed the court.

MARSHAL DE BROGLIE, commander of the royal troops.

CAMILLE DESMOULINS, a young barrister who incited the people to revolt.

JACQUES DE FLESSELLES, the senior city magistrate, murdered by the people.

MARQUIS DE LAUNAY, the elderly governor of the Bastille, who was also killed.

PIERRE HULIN, an ex-soldier, one of the two leaders of the attack on the Bastille.

LIEUTENANT ÉLIE, Queen's Infantry, who also led the attack on the Bastille.

ANNE ROBERT JACQUES TURGOT
JACQUES NECKER
CHARLES ALEXANDRE DE CALONNE
LOMÉNIE DE BRIENNE
} each in turn the controller-general of finance. These ministers tried to introduce reforms and end the threat of national bankruptcy.

BENJAMIN FRANKLIN, who was largely responsible for persuading the French to ally with the colonists in the American Revolution.

RÉVEILLON, an industrialist whose premises were ransacked.

JEAN SYLVAIN BAILLY, chairman of the National Assembly.

COMTE DE MIRABEAU, the deputy who defied the king and contended that the National Assembly was founded at the will of the people.

BARON DE BRETEUIL, the minister who threatened to burn down Paris.

MARQUIS DE LAFAYETTE, the man who demanded the convocation of the Estates-General.

The storming of the Bastille

THE DAY THE BASTILLE FELL

July 14, 1789
The Beginning of the End of the French Monarchy

By Douglas Liversidge

A World Focus Book

FRANKLIN WATTS, INC.
NEW YORK, 1972

Photographs courtesy of:
The Bettman Archive; page 35
United States Information Service; pages 17, 26, 27, 29
All others, including cover, courtesy of:
Bibliothèque Nationale, Paris

SBN 531-02155-6
Library of Congress Catalog Card Number: 74-183576
Printed in the United States of America
6 5 4 3 2 1

Contents

The Day the Bastille Fell

Paris was in ferment on the night of July 13, 1789.

A Capital in Ferment

When morning broke on the 14th of July, 1789, Paris was gripped with fear. The warm night had been filled with terror as citizens — some armed with cudgels and pikes — thronged the narrow, ill-lit streets. Many were ragged, their faces pinched with hunger. There were some who patrolled to protect life and property, but others were bent solely on plunder, taking advantage of the turmoil to get drunk, to steal, and to burn. A number were caught in lawless acts and quickly hanged. Passersby were beaten and robbed. Citizens listened in fear as bands, hammering on doors, demanded food, money, and arms.

For the poor, of course, food shortages and the high cost of bread were real concerns. Indeed, famine was far too threatening. That was why most of the customs posts had been set ablaze. With the tollgates gutted there would be no duty to pay on incoming goods. In the crude reasoning of the mob, that was the quickest way to lower the price of bread.

The people as a whole felt another anxiety. Near the city was the menacing threat of royal troops. And as darkness fell, the citizens expected an attack. In such a state of excitement, rumor soon took root. At two in the morning, disaster seemed imminent. It was said that thousands of soldiers were marching along the Rue Saint Antoine, the thoroughfare running past the Bastille, down to the Town Hall and the Place de Grève. It was false news, like other rumors that night. Yet it was enough to cause panic. Barricades hurriedly went up in the nearby streets.

For weeks, Paris had been in a state of unrest. The people of the city — indeed, of all France — had eagerly awaited the meeting of the Estates-General at Versailles. (The Estates-General was a governing body made up of three groups: the clergy, the nobles, and the people.) At last, it had seemed that the heavy burden of taxation would be shared by all, the many grievances remedied. But hope had faded, yielding to bitter frustration, then to violent anger. The reforms that were so badly needed seemed doomed. Then events moved swiftly. Defying Louis XVI, the people's deputies — called the Third Estate — created the National Assembly, pledging never to separate "until the constitution of the country shall have been established and founded on a solid base."

Louis XVI

This was a warning to the royal court. The old form of monarchy must go. So, too, must feudalism, which had long prevailed in France. Yet, at this stage the Third Estate had no desire to oust the king, provided that he worked for, and with, the people. As Jacques Necker, the controller-general of finance, had tactfully advised Louis, the time had come to forsake absolute rule and "deign to resign yourself to the English constitution."

But, stubbornly, Louis XVI had tried to keep all power within his grasp. As for his brothers and Queen Marie Antoinette, they were too arrogant and shortsighted to accept a compromise. Unwisely, Louis turned to them and the coterie they controlled. Thus, the court had plotted a show of military strength for mid-July.

"If it is necessary to burn Paris," Baron de Breteuil had boomed, "Paris will be burned." De Broglie promised to be just as ruthless. He assured the Prince de Condé, the king's brother, that grapeshot would quickly "disperse these argufiers and restore the absolute power which is going out, in place of the republican spirit which is coming in."

In the provinces, the troops, for the most part foreign mercenaries, were ordered to march on Paris and Versailles. The Assembly was to be dispersed and the capital ruthlessly brought to its senses.

Paris simmered with impending change and revolt — a revolt which would culminate in the storming of the ancient fortress-prison known as the Bastille. That act would change the future of France and the French people.

But what had brought it about? After centuries of monarchal rule, what had happened to cause people to turn so violently against it?

How It Began

Frenchmen had murmured their discontent even in the despotic days of Louis XIV, known as the Sun King, whose reign lasted seventy-three years, from 1643 to 1715. At the time of his death France was famine-stricken, its finances chaotic, its institutions weak or in ruins. The rumblings grew louder, especially toward the end of the reign of his great-grandson Louis XV (1715–74). The people were angered by the corruption and squandering of the royal court at Versailles. There the king was dissolute and idle, ignoring the poverty of his subjects, and interested solely in foreign affairs.

Most of the French aristocracy was in debt and, in many cases, dependent upon the court. This was in part the fault of the monarchy. When the Revolution confronted them after the Bastille fell, they were quite incapable of defending themselves.

Like the nobles, the upper clergy — the dignitaries and the religious houses — formed yet another privileged class. Both bred bitter resentment among the people, for as landholders they imposed a great financial burden, yet were themselves excused payment of the heaviest taxes. This privileged minority was the main cause of the Revolution and, when the storm broke, became its chief victim.

The miserable people were the peasants. That meant most Frenchmen. Of France's twenty-six million inhabitants at the time, less than two million lived in the towns. In the countryside hardships arose because too much land was overly subdivided. Moreover, in the main, knowledge and methods of farming were poor. The peasants also lacked good tools and, more important, capital to spend on the soil.

Famine often threatened, and sometimes struck, in wintertime. And when the winter was long, as in 1709 or at the beginning of the Revolution, the peasants' wretchedness was immense. Many died from cold and starvation.

France had functioned for centuries on a feudal system, although it was not strictly the feudalism of the Middle Ages. When it was ended on August 4, 1789, the body empowered to end it was called the Comité des Droits Féodaux (Committee on Feudal Rights).

Under the feudal system, rural France was mostly comprised of fiefs, or manorial estates, governed by lords. As a rule the lord exploited part of the fief and allowed his vassals to develop the rest.

In 1779, Louis XVI, son of Louis XV, eliminated *mainmorte*, or serfdom — which bound the peasant to the land — on the royal domains. Most lords had imitated him. Although the practice continued on some estates (chiefly those owned by the clergy), in 1788 only about 1,500,000 people (and perhaps less) were held by *mainmorte* throughout France. Since serfdom had almost vanished, the peasant could sell his land or hand it on to the person of his choice. Thus, although legally the peasant was only the tenant, he now considered himself the owner of the land he worked.

But whatever the class of peasant, all paid seignorial dues (to the lords). These varied among the manors, but no one could avoid them. They did, however, fall into disuse some years before the Revolution. They were entered in the *terriers*, or feudal regis-

In great contrast to the poverty of the peasants were the elaborate gardens of Versailles, the court of Louis XVI.

ters. To the lord also went personal rights and monopolies. Among these was forced labor. Dues were annual (paid in cash or kind). So-called casual taxes were imposed on the transfer of property and when land was sold or transferred through indirect inheritance.

A pamphlet, dated April 10, 1789, disclosed that "it was by means . . . of manorial law courts . . . that the lords had made themselves despots and held the inhabitants of the country districts in the chains of slavery." Even humble bequests were taxed, as were marriages, baptism, and burials.

And should the peasant's crops be good, he could not sell his grain for three months after the harvest. The lord of the manor alone was allowed to sell immediately, thus enabling him to do so at the best prices. There were also *banalités*, or tolls, for using the communal mill, bakehouse, or winepress. Tithes, too, contributed to the hardship. Each year a tithe, supposedly a tenth of the harvest, was allocated to the church, and the hospitals, universities, colleges, and schools administered by it. Whatever the amount, it undermined the peasant's income.

But tithes were only one aspect that the aristocracy — and ecclesiastical lords — aimed to exploit in the mid-eighteenth century. Affected by high prices and the depreciation of money, the upper classes engaged legal specialists to revive rights and dues that were mementoes of the feudal age. Not surprisingly, the peasants were incited to rid themselves of the feudal yoke.

The Peasants' Plight

Another factor compelled the peasants to rebel. Until the close of the seventeenth century, they had paid only one state tax, as well as the seignorial dues. This tax was the *taille,* from which the nobles and clergy were exempt. But owing to heavy expenses, primarily due to the crushing cost of war, Louis XIV and his successor burdened the people with more taxes. Burdensome, too, was the *capitation,* or poll tax, which was based on what a person earned. There were also taxes from customs duties and government monopolies — the *gabelle,* or salt tax, for example.

With justification, in the peasant's view this double onus was unfair. Why, he asked, should he pay dues and tithes to the local lord when he was also so heavily taxed by the state? Moreover, it was the state — not the nobles or clergy — who ran the main public services.

Because of the country's rural character, wealth in France really amounted to land ownership. This fell into three categories: communal estates; lands held by the nobles and clergy; and lands of the commoners. It has been estimated that in 1789 the aristocracy and ecclesiastics owned about 30 percent of the land. The soil not owned by them, and the communes as well, were cultivated by the bourgeoisie and the peasants.

By far the greatest inequalities were among the peasant landholders. Perhaps only about two million farmers could maintain themselves and their families on their land. As for most of the peasantry, each owned nothing more than a cottage and garden. When possible, these peasants rented land from the big owners. In the north of the country, such a peasant was known as a tenant farmer; in the south he was called a sharecropper.

In practice, most peasants had to work as farm laborers. But employment was seasonal, and often at the mercy of the elements. When bad weather ruined the crops, unemployment and distress were inescapable. And wintertime was always precarious; to follow a craft was the only way to eke out a paltry existence.

For many Frenchmen — including numerous small farmers — conditions worsened after about 1770. Over four decades the population had soared alarmingly, so that by 1789 it had grown by 80 percent in many areas. In some districts it had doubled. And at a time when peasants generally were striving to support larger families came a trend to create bigger farms by uniting smaller ones.

A resulting land shortage was inevitable. Consequently, there was a sharp rise in rents. Destitution was now the lot of the majority. Even for those who owned a few cattle, the right of free grazing was also vanishing, for the government was dividing up the common land. The lord was allowed one third; the rest went to the villagers in shares, depending on one's status. For the humblest peasant the portion was so slight that he had no option but to sell it, as well as his cattle.

Tragically, vast numbers of peasants were reduced to beggary. They took to the roads in thousands. Some burned charcoal in the forests, and sometimes reclaimed the land. In 1777, about 1,500,000 people were officially said to be vagrants. They left their homes, vainly seeking better fortune. When that eluded them, many formed armed bands, looting and tyrannizing the countryside. Others trekked to the towns, only to swell the numbers of the poor.

A City of Extremes

At the time of the Parisian uprising in July, 1789, the capital was the most populated center in France — some 600,000 citizens. Indeed, apart from London, it had the densest population in Europe. Further, it was socially a city of acute extremes. Roughly four-fifths of the people were the poverty-stricken — the apprentices, clerks, and other low wage earners; the remainder consisted of the well-to-do — the nobles, the clergy, and the *bourgeoisie*, or middle class.

In 1789, trade unionism did not apply to Parisian workers, for as yet there was no specific industry of any size. Prominent among the factories was the firm of Réveillon, which made printed wallpapers. Nearby stood the Santerre brewery. Spinning and cloth mills absorbed some of the capital's workers, as did the famous tapestry factory in the Gobelins area and the Paris Water Company in Chaillot.

But these, and other factories, were far outnumbered by little workshops. There master craftsmen employed journeymen and apprentices, and each craft was identified with its own district. When one spoke, for instance, of the Faubourg Saint Antoine, one immediately thought not only of the Bastille in the area, but of the many cabinetmakers, carpenters, and joiners. Tanners, cobblers, and shoemakers were peculiar to the Faubourgs Saint Victor, Saint Marcel, and Saint Denis. The quarters associated with goldsmiths,

The Gobelins area would become the scene of destruction.

jewelers, and clockmakers were the Place Dauphine, the Quai de l'Horloge, and the Quai des Orfèvres.

In these densely thronged neighborhoods festered the rebellious, inflammatory element that was rivaled only by the workers of the markets — the Halles. There the notorious fishwives were ever ready to participate in street upheavals.

In Paris wages differed sharply among the various trades. In 1789, for example, a locksmith received up to fifty *sous* daily, but an unskilled laborer earned roughly half that sum. This was strikingly below the rising cost of living, due especially to the high price of bread, an item which often absorbed about half of a worker's expenses.

During the four decades preceding the fall of the Bastille, workers had often struck to gain higher wages. In fact, the hatters were on strike in June, 1789, not long before the Bastille was besieged. But increases were low and destitution commonplace. Indeed, in 1789 the vagrants and the workless in Paris totaled more than thirty thousand; about fourteen thousand occupied the hospital wards.

In these frightful conditions, a rise in the price of bread could be an explosive factor. A bread shortage could excite passions just as much, often ending in riots. A minimum of one million loaves was needed daily for Paris. This in itself involved a detailed system of administration and a close scrutiny of the grain trade.

Grain not needed locally within an area ten leagues wide around Paris was sent to the capital by producers or accredited merchants. The bigger merchants also bought from the provinces as well as abroad. The grain was conveyed to more than four thousand mills around the city. Then the flour, checked at the customs posts, was sent to the Halles. There it was bought by both the city and the itinerant bakers and by the *faubourgs*. Of all the capital's bread markets, the most vital was at the Halles. The police daily noted the stock of loaves there, realizing that an uprising might occur if the shortage was acute.

At the time of the Bastille incident, Paris was a city of festering discontent. But resentment was not confined to the workers. The bourgeoisie on the whole disliked the nobles. France's industrial progress in the eighteenth century could be attributed chiefly to the middle class. The French bourgeoisie was also educated and

14

affluent, but it had little chance of serving in either the government or the administration. That was the prerogative of the lords — to the extreme annoyance of the bourgeoisie.

Times had certainly changed. In the seventeenth century most *Parlements* (courts of justice) had even been ready to admit commoners, but now the aristocracy kept membership to themselves. This applied just as much to the hierarchies of the church and the military. Grievances, therefore, tended to drive the bourgeoisie closer to the peasantry (from which many had come), especially to a new small class of peasants who, despite the unhappy lives of peasants generally, were getting richer. This phenomenon was inclined to occur where the power of a noble was on the wane. The voices of these peasants eventually cried out for the abolition of feudal rights. And like the bourgeoisie, they, too, were influenced by a third force — the writers — which sought the death of the old régime.

Power of the Pen

Louis XIV had destroyed liberty in France. But in the eighteenth century, men took up the pen in protest. They attacked the Church, the traditions of the nobles, and even the learning of the lawyers. More than anyone else, they encouraged free thought among those classes barred from the spheres of government.

The authors themselves received their first impulses from England. For instance, the lawyer Charles de Secondat Montesquieu (1689–1755) recommended political liberty on English lines and advocated English constitutionalism in place of despotism in France.

Voltaire (1694–1778), with views molded by John Locke, the English philosopher, urged tolerance and freedom of thought and conscience. Early in his literary career, Voltaire, who had been educated by Jesuits, attacked the priesthood. His book *Henriade* praised Britain's Henry IV at the expense of Louis XIV. Voltaire lived in England for three years and returned to France imbued with English humanitarianism. His criticisms of the French court led him to settle at Ferney, near Genevan territory, so that he could cross the frontier into Switzerland should there be fear of arrest. Voltaire had known imprisonment in the Bastille, the first time as a young man of twenty-two, after writing Latin verse which ridiculed the regent and his daughter. His second sentence had been preceded by a beating, instigated by the aristocrat de Rohan-Chabot, who had been the object of Voltaire's wit.

Now removed from Paris, Voltaire directed the defense of the oppressed. He encouraged the men who, following the writers in natural science, wrote their great dictionary, the *Encyclopédie*. The encyclopedists visualized a new type of society, condemning such things as organized religion, war, and inequality of taxation. Denis Diderot (1713–84), the chief editor, corrected proofs of the *Encyclopédie* while imprisoned in the castle at Vincennes.

Jean-Jacques Rousseau (1712–78), a Genevan clockmaker's

Voltaire is shown blessing the grandson of Benjamin Franklin.

son, addressed himself to the sympathies of the people. He became the foremost teacher of those who carried out the French Revolution. Tutor, secretary, and music teacher, among various occupations, Rousseau was accepted by Diderot as a contributor to the *Encyclopédie*. Yet, when he quarreled with the editor, he became as intolerant of the encyclopedists as he was of the established church.

Of Rousseau's books, the one which most influenced society was *The Social Contract*. It was a revelation of a new code of politics, in which he vigorously affirmed the sovereignty of the people. To Rousseau all men were equal and all were born free.

When many people were already hostile to France's ruling régime, such a book was bound to make men think, if not stir up social strife. People, Rousseau considered, should be allowed to develop naturally in whatever way led to the greatest progress. Briefly, nature should replace the rigid teaching of the schoolmaster. Moreover, the priest and the philosopher should be kept apart from the training of people.

His book *Héloise* dealt with the moral code of mankind. He, too, appealed to man's conscience and sense of right against the selfish immoralities of the day. Aware of these evils, many people enthusiastically accepted Rousseau's ideas and desired a revolution in morals as well as in religion and politics.

Thus, the work of the philosophers undermined the old institutions which, it was claimed, enslaved men. It demanded equality among all men and obedience to the law irrespective of birth. Feudalism must end, to be replaced by a freedom of contract between men. Although the philosophers may have had little influence on the illiterate peasants, they awoke in the more educated middle class a realization of their rights.

These were the troubled times in which Louis XVI came to the throne. His grandfather, Louis XV, had been aware of the coming social outburst. But, selfishly, certain that it would not happen in his lifetime, he had cared little for the plight of France or for the plight of his grandson.

In 1770, the young Louis had married Marie Antoinette, the daughter of Maria Theresa, archduchess of Austria. In temperament and personality the couple contrasted vividly — a contrast which would eventually cause their destruction. Louis's kindliness can now be seen as weakness, and his simplicity was, in fact, stupidity. He was noted for his obstinacy, but basically he was not firm. Moreover, his good and bad qualities left him bewildered when trying to cope with his tottering régime. When the Bastille fell, he is credited with the remark, "Why, it's a revolt!" to which the Duc de La Rochefoucauld-Liancourt explained, "No, sire, it's a revolution." This may be a legendary story, but it is in keeping with the unfortunate king. His main obsession, even in times of crisis, was the hunt.

Marie Antoinette was quite different. She possessed much of the high spirits of her empress-mother. Frenchmen always treated her as a foreigner, but during her earlier years at court she had won

Queen Marie Antoinette

their chivalry because of her beauty. Then she came between the king and his efforts to ease the misery of his people. She created a court party of her own, interfering with the choice of ministers, and she angered the starving people by her unbridled extravagances. With foolish recklessness, she induced the king to depend on foreign aid.

Rioting for Bread

Louis's reign began with promise in 1774 because he entrusted the key office of controller-general of finance to a far-sighted economist, Anne Robert Jacques Turgot (1727–81). It was an unusual choice, for Turgot's middle-class background was bound to rouse the hostility of the aristocracy and the court.

At first, it seemed as if Louis would support his minister's proposals — economic changes and the abolition of privilege. The state, asserted Turgot, who was a friend and admirer of Voltaire, should spend less and should draw its money from all classes of society, including the nobles and clergy. As an example to others, he refused his own salary. But the privileged were immediately hostile, claiming that this was an intrusion into their traditional rights.

At the end of September, 1774, Turgot introduced free trade in grain and flour, believing that this would be to the benefit of France. But prices rose. Various views circulated as to the cause. Some contended that powerful interests had revived the Famine Pact, the grain ring that had been set up with the approval and participation of Louis XV, and which had caused starvation among the poor. Others — particularly the middle class, who were inclined to favor Turgot — argued that a bad harvest was the cause.

Whatever the reason, rioting — which came to be known as the *Guerre des Farines,* or Flour War — broke out in the markets

21

of Paris and other parts of France. The first disturbance occurred in Dijon on April 18, 1775, where a miller named Carre, accused of hoarding, had to climb to the roof of a lawyer's house to evade the mob. But the rioters ransacked his home and destroyed his flour.

Thousands of angry citizens even demonstrated before the palace at Versailles. They shouted for a decrease in the price of grain, and the governor of Versailles, the Prince de Poix, fixed the price according to the crowd's demands. Then, early in May, bakeries were pillaged in Paris. A contemporary account says: "The mob, which had collected under the instigation of gangs of ruffians and bandits . . . ran riot at the Halles and plundered the bakers' shops. Unrest spread quickly throughout the city center and the suburbs. . . . The mob attempted to ransack the Corn Market and tear open all the sacks of flour; but fortunately they were unable to achieve their object; they made up for it by visiting all the markets and forcing the bakers to hand over their bread, as well as private individuals who happened to have some in store and whose doors were broken down if they showed the slightest reluctance to open them."

Over 400 people were arrested; 162 were prosecuted. Two of the leaders were hanged in the Place de Grève. In the main, the insurgents were vagabonds and members of the working class, such as ragmen, carpenters, and apprentices — in short, the sort of people who would later attack the Bastille.

Turgot stoically refused to give way, swiftly organizing two armies to maintain order. Voltaire and others believed the finance minister to be the victim of a secret plot planned by the nobles and clergy. Yet, it is possible that the high prices were the offspring of poor harvests in 1770, 1772, and 1774. These unfortunately coincided with a decisive rise in the population. There would be more

22

riots in the coming years — a prelude to the storming of the Bastille and the French Revolution.

An able administrator, Turgot sincerely tried to remedy the evils of the day. The more intelligent members of the middle class appreciated this and welcomed his ideas. But the privileged instinctively turned against him and finally were overwhelming. The king dismissed him in 1776, plaintively observing, "Turgot and I are the only men in France who care for the people."

Necker and Franklin

Like Turgot, Jacques Necker (1732–1804), a Genevan banker who took control of the nation's treasury in July, 1777, was acutely aware of the need for drastic reform. Necker has been described as a charlatan, but he knew that the years of royal despotism were limited. Necker realized that the French monarchy had one chance for survival: to accept a constitutional form of government with national representation in a parliament on the English pattern. But to Necker the king crisply observed, "It is of the essence of my authority not to be an intermediary, but to be at the head."

As a first step toward representative government, Necker recommended the setting up of provincial assemblies. Next, there would be representative government of the entire country. In that new political pattern, all propertied classes would form the French parliament. Even if the king valued the wisdom of Necker's scheme, after founding a few provincial assemblies he abandoned the plan. Again, he had wilted before the pressures of the aristocracy.

That was the thorniest problem of all: to meet the great expenses of the administration without undermining the traditional rights of the nobles and the clergy. Despite the enormous national debt, Necker kept the machinery of government in motion. But he failed to change the selfish outlook of the privileged. In the end their attitude would bring about their own destruction.

Before his dismissal in 1781, Necker stirred the nation by

24

Jacques Necker

issuing his *Compte rendu*. This was an account of the country's money and the way it was spent. He wanted to tell the people the truth, to reveal the actual financial state of France. Never before had the royal government been so exposed. The *Compte rendu* even gave details of the cost of the court.

Necker's accounting, however, was wrong. He reported a credit of ten million *livres* when there was a deficit of nearly five times that sum. And before the end of the American Revolution (1775–83), in which France aided the colonists against England, the deficit would grow to more than a billion livres.

Curiously, Louis XVI had agreed to let Necker publish the *Compte rendu*. This in itself seemed revolutionary, for it laid bare the moneyed classes and their way of spending. Necker had, therefore, assaulted the tradition of privilege, but it would cause his

25

downfall. That the king should keep accounts and let them be put before the people was, to the aristocracy, akin to treason.

Necker's motives, however, had been different. By being frank with the nation he had hoped to win the people's confidence. For, oddly enough, by a proper handling of the money there was hope for the future. France was growing richer in a commercial sense. As one English contemporary recorded, "The advance of maritime commerce has been more rapid in France than in England. Commerce has doubled in twenty years."

But the court party, led by the queen, would not tolerate Necker's kind of intrusion, and he was compelled to resign.

The American Revolution was to be a major factor in the affairs of France. Indeed, the subsequent alliance had a twofold

Farmers battling British troops at Concord, to begin the American Revolution

The American Declaration of Independence inspired the French to strive for liberty.

effect. To begin with, war with England became inevitable. Also, the expense was so great that it completed the financial ruin of the old régime and hastened its destruction. France, for instance, had to build a fleet to challenge England on the seas. That was costly. Next, the revolt of the English colonies and the Constitution of the new United States stimulated the revolutionary spirit in France. The Declaration of Independence of the colonists influenced its counterpart in France. Soon after the Bastille fell, the Constitutional Committee of the National Assembly met to consider the Declaration of the Rights of Man, and it took the American charter as its guide.

One person who helped to draft the American Declaration did more than any other to cement the Franco-American alliance. In doing so he left his mark on the destiny of France. He was Benjamin Franklin.

While serving as agent for the American colonies in London, this amiable, humorous man first visited France in the autumn of 1767. He endeared himself to many. On returning to Philadelphia in 1775, he prepared the colonists' appeal for aid from the French king. Furthermore, he wrote the instructions for Silas Deare, the member of Congress who was to convey it.

Franklin was also elected a delegate from Philadelphia to the conference that formally renounced in the name of the American colonies all allegiance to King George III and called for an election of delegates to form a constitutional government for the United Colonies. Next, with four others, Franklin collaborated in drawing up the Declaration of Independence.

In September of that year, after encouraging news had arrived from France, Congress chose Franklin to be one of three to journey to the French court to solicit the support of France. He sailed with two grandsons in the *Reprisal*, a sloop of war, reaching Nantes on December 7, and Paris at the end of the month. For his residence, he rented a house in Passy, then a suburb of the capital, and owned by a supporter of the American cause — Le Ray de Chaumont, who had influence at court.

Franklin, the scientist and politician, was hailed in France with enthusiasm. Schlosser, the German historian, wrote: "Franklin's appearance in the French saloons, even before he began to negotiate, was an event of great importance to the whole of Europe."

During his third year in Paris, writing to his daughter about a medallion of himself, Franklin explained: "A variety of others have been made since, of different sizes; some to be set in the lids of snuff-boxes and some so small as to be worn in rings, and the numbers sold are incredible. These with the pictures, busts, and prints . . . have made your father's face as well known as the moon, so that he durst not do anything that would oblige him to run away, as his phiz would discover him wherever he should venture to show it."

This runaway son of a Boston candlemaker was lionized

Lafayette with George Washington at Mount Vernon

throughout France. Streets and societies were named after him. But, more important, his simple yet magnetic personality animated Frenchmen to support the rebel cause. He signed for the United States the treaty whereby France agreed to enter the American war. In February, 1779, the Marquis de Lafayette, then a general with the colonists' forces, brought a commission from the American Congress to Franklin as sole plenipotentiary of the United States to the Court of France.

The success of Franklin's diplomacy was mirrored by the sums of money supplied by the French government to the colonists. Between 1777 and 1782, some twenty-six million francs were secured, although the country was virtually bankrupt and Necker keenly opposed it. Franklin doubtless instilled a revolutionary spirit in Frenchmen. Indeed, among those who attacked the Bastille were men who had fought in the American war. And when Franklin had the American Constitution translated into French, many more were inspired by a new sense of liberty.

It is one of the ironies of history that, to sap the strength of rival England, the French court contributed toward the founding of the American Republic, and, in the process, further sapped its own resources and helped to create republican France.

Calonne and the Notables

After Necker's departure, Louis XVI was completely dominated by the queen. Joli de Fleury, who followed Necker, was noted for mismanagement. D'Ormesson, who replaced him, was no more competent. When he resigned office, there was the equivalent of about £14,400 in the treasury, after borrowing almost £14 million sterling in two and a half years.

Charles Alexandre de Calonne (1734–1802), known at court as "the Ladies' Minister," was the choice of Marie Antoinette. Here was someone who would pander to her extravagances. Not that there was much to lavish on the court. It is said that Calonne found "two little bags of gold with 1,200 francs in each" in the royal treasury. He later observed: "There was neither money nor credit; the current debts of the Crown were immense, the income pledged far in advance, the resources dried up, public property valueless, the coin of the realm impoverished and withdrawn from circulation — the whole, in a word, on the very verge of bankruptcy."

Tragically for the country, Calonne had no experience as a financier and perhaps no great regard for France. His primary concern was to cater to the queen's whims, such as gambling; nothing must detract from the gaiety of the court.

Thus, the annual deficit continued to grow. The people groaned under the load of taxation, and anger smoldered. Their hatred for the queen, whom they nicknamed "Madame Deficit," got

31

worse. In Paris, the enmity intensified when a new wall went up around the city. Calonne allowed it to be built to simplify the collection of tolls at the fifty-four gates. As was expected, a rise in prices was the outcome.

France was hurrying toward ruin. In the autumn of 1786, even Calonne saw at last that the country must choose between total bankruptcy or a drastic reform of the tax system. But, petted by both court and nobles, Calonne knew just how delicate was the subject of reform. It would displease not only the privileged but also the Parlements, who by tradition supported the aristocrats and their feudal rights.

And so Calonne resorted to a practice which had been adopted at other times in the history of France. He would outline his plan for reform to a gathering of selected nobles — an Assembly of Notables. Louis XVI backed the idea, the essence of which was that all Frenchmen would be equal under taxation.

Before the notables at Versailles on February 22, 1787, Calonne summarized the state of the treasury. For forty years, he pointed out, financial affairs had grown steadily worse. The deficit, which had started in 1739, had now reached alarming proportions. Calonne quoted figures in support of this, warning that France verged on ruin. That meant disaster for the privileged as well.

In spite of this stern warning, the nobles were heedless. They clung stubbornly to the past, opposing Calonne's desire to levy land tax equally on everyone. Calonne wanted to have the taille reduced and internal customs barriers ended. Forced labor should also disappear. There should be free trade in grain as well, he said, to prevent the Famine Pact from recurring.

Calonne annoyed the nobles, more so by attempting to revive Necker's scheme of provincial assemblies. These, elected by landowners of all classes, would assess direct taxation. Another incursion into feudal rights was an offer to buy back seignorial dues collected by the Church.

The notables accepted very little. They would agree to provincial assemblies only if the privileged had a majority vote. In that way they would retain power. During March the Assembly consented to reduce the taille and suppress forced labor, but would not interfere with the land tax — the basis of Calonne's proposals. Other efforts by Calonne to effect reform only roused the Assembly to criticize the government.

Faced with this impasse, Calonne asked Louis XVI to dissolve the Assembly. But, again, reactionary forces were too strong. Some nobles, with the help of the queen, persuaded the king, instead, to dismiss his finance minister.

Calonne had pleased no one. Even the people condemned him, for they wrongly assumed that the Assembly's objective was to introduce new taxes rather than to discuss reforms.

The Parlements Oppose
the Court

One of Calonne's most vehement critics had been Loménie de Brienne (1727–94), archbishop of Toulouse. After Bouvard de Fourqueux's brief period in office, Brienne — again the queen's nominee — took control as "principal minister." He soon found out how imperative had been Calonne's proposals. The privileged classes must accept reform if France was to avert national bankruptcy. Brienne demanded that both nobles and clergy pay their share of the land tax. He knew that in so doing a critical situation would arise throughout France.

The crisis was not long in coming, and from this time on, the court's power would begin to wane. Parties formed for the struggle over this heatedly contested issue. For the tax were the king, queen, Brienne, and some nobles. Opposing were Louis Philippe Joseph, Duc d'Orléans — whose shadow was spreading over the political scene — and most of the aristocracy. Supporting Orléans and his followers was the Parlement of Paris, for the lawyers defended privilege. And witnessing this political maneuvering were the hungry people.

In this period, Louis XVI made one of the most unwise decisions of his reign. He probably could have won over the people had he shown any taste for reform. Acceptance of constitutional rule would perhaps have saved the monarchy. But he, too, held tenaciously to outdated privileges. Driven on by his frivolous queen,

Louis Philippe Joseph, Duc d'Orléans

he sought only to save the ancient monarchy. To achieve this he was willing to sacrifice the nobles. This attitude was mutual. In the end, both would be destroyed.

Basically, Louis XVI wished to do his best for France, but he listened to the wrong counsel. He was also too weak to cope with the revolution that began to loom. The people themselves were unconcerned about the rights and wrongs of either faction. They were interested only in their own claims against both.

When Brienne demanded the land tax for all, the notables argued that they lacked the power to approve it. Only the country's accredited representatives were so empowered. This cunning move was followed on May 21, 1787, by a demand which was to change French history. Lafayette insisted on "the convocation of a truly national assembly." When the king's brother, the Comte d'Artois,

35

asked Lafayette to be more precise, he answered: "The Estates-General of the kingdom."

The Estates-General, which consisted of three groups, or estates — the clergy, the nobles, and the people — were august bodies which had not functioned since 1614. That was 173 years earlier. The last meeting had broken up in confusion.

Lafayette's demand must have caught Louis XVI unawares. At least, he made no hasty decision. He dismissed the Assembly of Notables four days after Lafayette's request, for one thing was abundantly clear — the aristocracy, by and large, was willing to undermine the throne to safeguard itself.

Therefore, in a sense revolt had begun — not so much by the people but among the nobles. Another fact that had emerged from the Assembly's deliberations was that the land tax could be imposed on the aristocracy only by force.

Under the law of France, the king's edicts had to be registered by the Parlement of Paris before they could be enforced. Brienne now submitted the draft bills which had been presented to the Assembly. The Parlement's reaction echoed that of the nobles. When asked to register an equal distribution of the land tax and an increased stamp duty, the lawyers refused. They claimed, like the Assembly, to be incompetent to approve taxes, and they renewed the demand that the Estates-General be convoked. And so, in desperation, the court resorted to force.

On August 6, 1787, the king held a great *lit de justice,* or personal visitation to the Parlement, to enforce registration. But the next day the Parlement declared the registration illegal and void. On August 13 it further antagonized the king, declaring the edicts to be "contrary to the rights of the nation." The king retaliated by exiling the Parlement to Troyes.

36

If this measure hoped to win popular support, the king had erred badly. Although the people were anxious for reforms, oddly enough it was the Parlement that won the popular voice. The more progressive spirits would not accept as sufficient the reforms recommended by the queen's party. In the capital the Chambres des Comptes (Audit Office) and the Cour des Aides (which assessed subsidies) dissociated themselves from Brienne's bills, although they had earlier approved them.

Rioting broke out in the streets, and the home of the commissioner of police was looted. Pamphlets, some vulgar and abusive, campaigned against the king, queen, and the government. More opposition came from the provincial supreme courts. Seemingly alarmed by this reaction, the government gave way. The edicts concerning land tax and stamp duty were withdrawn, and the Parlement was asked merely to consent to a temporary increase in a tax

Brienne's effigy is burned by the mob.

called the *vingtieme,* or twentieth. This was agreed to, and the Parlement was welcomed back in Paris on September 28.

The crowds were jubilant, rioting in protest against the government. Both police and troops were assaulted with fireworks and stones. The Comtesse de Polignac, an intimate of the queen's, was hung in effigy. Only when the Parlement asked for it did order return.

Yet, there was another outburst some weeks later. This time it was the middle class that vented its wrath. The Parlement, hailed as "the defenders of the people," now grew more brazen in its attitude toward the court. Desperately Brienne pleaded with certain members of the Parlement. In secret negotiations, he sought approval for a huge loan to be raised over the next five years. In return he would persuade the king to convoke the Estates-General at the end of that period — in 1792.

On November 19, 1787, the king and Parlement met at a "royal session" (which was less provocative than a *lit de justice*). Yet, there appeared to be no attempt to suppress ill feeling. Louis XVI obstinately refused to surrender any of the monarchy's rights. And his demand that Protestants be given all civic rights was bound, if not calculated, to annoy. The Parlement, in turn, hotly criticized the government's financial policy. This, however, did not deter the king from asking for 420 million livres, an enormous sum in those times.

The king promised to convoke the Estates-General in 1789. Then he ordered the Parlement to register the edict and sanction the loans. It was a dramatic moment. "It's illegal," protested the Duc d'Orléans. His condemnation seemed well justified when the king retorted, "I don't care." He quickly added, "It's legal since I wish it." The meeting ended in chaos.

38

By order of the king, Orléans was exiled the next day, but he had succeeded in damaging the monarch's authority. Passions ran high throughout France. All the Parlements were at once in conflict with the government. They were also guilty of double-dealing. Secretly they were striving to transfer the control of France to the privileged classes, while posing as the people's champion.

On May 3, 1788, the Parlement of Paris bluntly asserted that only the Estates-General could vote subsidies and taxes. Furthermore, Frenchmen could no longer be arbitrarily arrested or detained. This meant that no one could be imprisoned purely on the strength of a royal warrant. Moreover, no one could sit in judgment other than an accredited magistrate. As for the provinces, all customs and privileges could not be changed. Cleverly, the lawyers were automatically protecting the nobles' interests.

The National Party Emerges

As Louis XVI rightly observed, if he yielded, "the monarchy would become nothing but an aristocracy of magistrates." But what action could he take? The government's weakness was already manifest to everyone. However, there was still room to maneuver. The king and the government locked the doors of the Palais de Justice, where the Parlement sat. To its surprise, the Parlement of Paris was "imprisoned" for the night, and two of its more ebullient members found themselves arrested. Then, on May 8, the king issued six edicts virtually stripping the Parlements of their power.

In their place would function courts called *grands bailliages*. As for the edicts, in the future these would be registered by a plenary court. The reason for this step soon became clear — it had the end of feudalism as its target. The king, rather belatedly, was beginning to do what others had suggested since the time of Turgot. But was he too late?

The seignorial courts were now seriously threatened. In the future, any participant in a civil action could request that the case be heard by a royal justice.

As the court no doubt anticipated, the nobility was incensed. But, rather unexpectedly, so too was the middle class, which did not think that the reforms reached far enough.

Neither view worried the mass of the people. Their agitation sprang from the critical harvest of 1788, for the cost of living was rising at a deplorable rate. In Paris hunger was rife, and unemployment was catastrophic among the rapidly growing population. The conditions were ripe for revolt.

In the capital the mob went wild. Outbreaks erupted in other parts of France. There were demonstrations and rioting, and the *grands bailliages* were the objects of ruthless attacks. Incidents were many. At Pau, rioting peasants used force to return the Parlement to its former status. In Dauphine — and particularly at Grenoble — the insurrection took on a more violent aspect. When the Comte de Clermont-Tonnerre, the military commander, announced the dissolving of the Parlement, the people rebelled. As the tocsin (alarm bell) rang, peasants hurried to Grenoble from neighboring villages. There, harangued by agitators, passions overcame reason. Suddenly, shots were fired, and people died in a bloody clash with the troops. The defiant mob, however, broke into the commander's palace, and, with an ax poised over his head, Cleremont-Tonnerre yielded to force and revoked the king's edicts.

There were other uprisings — in Provence, Languedoc, Rousillon, Flanders, and Burgundy. Brienne, in despair, saw his policy a shambles. Submitting to popular will, he announced that the king would convoke the Estates-General for May 1, 1789. On August 24, Brienne resigned.

His departure was the excuse for more fireworks and demonstrations in the streets. On August 29, the guards' posts on the Pont Neuf were set ablaze. In trying to restore order, the soldiers killed rioters in the Place de Grève. And when Lamoignon, the minister of justice, resigned in mid-September, the people again ran wild. They tried to gut the homes of Lamoignon and Brienne and attacked the house of Chevalier Dubois, commandant of the Paris Guard.

The guardroom on the Pont Neuf is set on fire.

The nobles, who had much to gain from this ferment, also allied with the Parlements. In Britanny, twelve delegates were chosen to convey the nobles' protests to the king. But instead of receiving them, Louis consigned the delegates to the Bastille. Finally, on July 30 the king agreed to meet eighteen delegates, but he insisted that they must represent the three estates.

Suspecting the king's motive, the Breton nobles decided on a plan of their own. They founded correspondence committees, imitating the former rebels in the American colonies. At Rennes, where there had been rioting, a central body was created to oppose the edicts.

Out of the chaos and strife emerged an organization which was to influence future events. Including such people as lawyers, philosophers, journalists, and certain liberal nobles, it was called the national or patriot party. From this body would rise eminent figures of the French Revolution. Not only did this movement dissociate itself from the Parlements, but it replaced the Parlements in the vanguard of revolutionary elements.

Uprisings and the Elections

Meanwhile, the popular Necker was recalled, much to the reluctance of Marie Antoinette, who loathed him. This step would reduce the king's power, but the queen wrote that it was "very essential that he [Necker] should accept. The king fully agrees with me. . . . I fear that we may be compelled to nominate a prime minister."

Necker's recall was received by the people with excitement. At last, they thought, here was someone who would check the rise in the price of bread. Necker won even more respect by lending two million livres to the country from his personal fortune. This act set an example to others and enabled him to raise loans which would ward off bankruptcy until the Estates-General met the following May.

But now provocative questions arose. In what proportion were the deputies, or representatives, to be appointed to the three estates? What was to be the constitution and general form? The aristocracy, naturally anxious to retain its feudal privileges, wished to stick with the old pattern of 1614. The Parlement of Paris, with its lawyerlike preference for precedent over justice, supported them. Quickly the widespread esteem that the Parlements had wrongly enjoyed disappeared. They were now seen to be as zealous for privilege as the nobles themselves.

In contrast, the middle class and the richer peasants were for change. They claimed a preponderance of numbers and wealth. The Third Estate, they argued, should, therefore, be composed of as many members as the other two estates combined. Furthermore, at the meeting every shred of privilege should be abolished and the three orders should debate and vote by head and not by body. Obviously, if the voting was by body, then the clergy and nobles could always outvote the people two to one. In that way they would retain their privileges.

But the people were determined to end all that. And the patriot party was equally emphatic on the point. Its members met in such places as reading-rooms and masonic lodges, and in the manner of the American insurgents and the Breton nobles, they set up correspondence committees to advance their claims. From the printing presses poured pamphlets and the earliest revolutionary periodicals.

Because the court had to be impartial, Necker entrusted the delicate matter of deciding on numbers and voting procedure to a second Assembly of Notables. As might be expected, a majority voted in favor of the clergy and nobles. But the patriot party was adamant, demanding that its claims be met.

The country seethed with propaganda that smacked of revolution. The harassed aristocracy, now the victim of the unrest it had fostered in recent months, pleaded anxiously with Artois and Condé, the princes, to intercede with the king. They would accept their share of taxation if the Third Estate was deprived of a majority of deputies.

Necker, however, was well aware of the people's mood. He induced Louis to concede to the Third Estate.

The unrest which troubled France in the months that preceded the Estates-General did not come solely from political bickering.

The elections were held when famine threatened. This catastrophe owed its origin to the calamitous harvest of 1788. A terrible hailstorm had laid waste the fields in the country's best corn-growing lands, around Paris. There was also the Eden Treaty, which allowed British goods to pour into France. In return, Britain reduced the duty on French wines, but it so happened that the British preferred to drink Portuguese wines.

Perhaps French industry was affected more by the scarcity of money. Most Frenchmen had to cope first with the shocking cost of food. Unemployment was widespread and bread was scarce and costly. And, rightly or wrongly, the poor people blamed the government for both, accusing it and the producers of hoarding grain. A severe winter made everything worse.

Before the Bastille fell, there would be many more uprisings in France. The disturbances followed much the same pattern. Carrying knives, cudgels, and scythes, the peasants would enter the nearest town, compelling the people in the markets to sell at low prices. Sometimes they seized the grain, sharing it among themselves and promising to refund the cost after the next harvest. Some of the hungry plundered granaries and convoys of corn. Angry bands seized grain in the villages, and even compelled some lords to abolish all feudal rights. Others raided bakeries and grain-chandlers' shops. Many refused to pay tithes and dues — even the taxes. The cry for liberty was now more frequent.

Villagers in the valley of the Vance took back the grain they had paid in feudal dues. At Manosque the people rioted and stoned the bishop, accusing him of supporting hoarders. At Chateaux, monasteries and mills were attacked and pillaged. At Limoux, a disorderly crowd entered the tax-collector's office and threw the account books into the River Aude.

Insurrection gained impetus because the soldiers suppressed it only halfheartedly, if at all. Many had fought alongside the American insurgents and were in sympathy with the people. It was the middle class that took action as anarchy grew. In some places they hurriedly formed their own militia, as in Paris before the siege of the Bastille.

Polling in Paris

In this tense and turbulent atmosphere, the elections for the Estates-General took place. They concluded at the polls in Paris, which now swarmed with desperate newcomers from the countryside.

To qualify as an elector or a deputy in the Paris elections, one had to be of French nationality and over twenty-five years of age (as in the provinces). But in the capital it was also imperative to furnish evidence of a university degree, a diploma of mastership, a civil function, a public office, or proof of assessment for a poll tax of over six livres. This, therefore, deprived the greater percentage of the lower classes of the vote and of attendance at meetings.

For the purpose of choosing the deputies of the Third Estate, Paris was divided into sixty districts. Electoral assemblies were convened in each. In the end, representatives were chosen from the bourgeoisie — lawyers and tradesmen predominating. Not unnaturally, the poorer people, who were numerically greater, were aggrieved. Even some members of the middle class were in sympathy, and pamphlets were issued in protest. Typical is this extract: "Why is this immense class, made up of journeymen and wage-earners, the focus of all political revolutions, this class which has so many protests to make, the only protests which deserve, only too well, the degrading name of *doléances* [grievances], cast out from the bosom of the nation? Why has this order no representatives of its own? . . . Why is it the only order which, in accordance with the

47

old tyrannical customs of bygone barbarous and ignorant days, is not summoned to the national assembly, and is treated with as much scorn as injustice?"

This seemed contrary to the Decree in Council of July 5, 1788, which was supposed to allow all citizens to participate in the drawing up of *cahiers*, or grievances and proposals. In that way all classes of society were to submit their views on how the country should be reorganized.

The Réveillon Affair

The preparation of the *cahiers* at the electoral assembly of the Sainte Marguerite district on April 23, 1789, led to the worst riot in Paris prior to the Bastille incident. A rich industrialist named Réveillon, of the Faubourg Saint Antoine, told a gathering that bread was the foundation of the national economy. They should insist, he said, that the fruit of one's labors should no longer have its price settled at the gates of Paris. When, he contended, satisfaction had been secured on that point, the employers could proceed to a gradual reduction of their workmen's wages. That, in turn, would yield a gradual reduction in the price of manufactured articles.

Réveillon, it has been said, had no desire to lower the standard of living of the workers, and, in fact, had recommended other reductions. But the workers did not consider these. All that mattered to them was that Réveillon wished to lower wages. Indeed, this appeared to be in the minds of other employers. For instance, Henriot, owner of a saltpeter factory, had spoken in a similar vein at the assembly of the Enfants-Trouvés district, also in the Faubourg Saint Antoine.

Whatever Réveillon's motive, the subject of lower wages at a time of hunger and unemployment lacked wisdom. The Faubourg Saint Antoine was one of the most densely populated sections of Paris. Besides the normal inhabitants, there had been an influx of unemployed. Thiroux de Crosne, lieutenant of police, gave this

49

ominous warning: "We have in the Faubourg Saint Antoine more than 40,000 workmen. The high price of bread and other commodities might give rise to disturbances in this *faubourg*, where there has already been some unrest."

Saint Antoine drew the unemployed — at this time mostly the starving jobless from the countryside — because the normally all-powerful guilds were less strong there. Many people had no link with the guilds and worked for themselves in their homes. Factories such as Réveillon's were independent of the guilds as well.

As for Réveillon, although he was demanding and severe, he paid high wages. He, too, had been a worker. But this former apprentice papermaker, then journeyman, had quit his guild to manufacture wallpaper — a new and lucrative trend — on his own. His factory occupied the entire ground floor of Titonville, a house so vast that it had brought disaster to the financier who built it. Réveillon had purchased these premises, as well as Titon's lavish furniture, and used the second floor as his residence.

All accounts imply that Réveillon was a cultured man, and had accumulated a magnificent library of more than 50,000 books. Four years before the Réveillon affair disrupted his life, he had received the award presented by Necker for "the encouragement of the useful arts." Actually, Réveillon's commercial activities were an asset to France. His exports were substantial.

When everything is considered, the subsequent riots seem out of proportion to the remarks he made. The fury of the workers, therefore, rather mirrors the acute tension at the time and the dread of famine.

The lieutenant of police expected mob violence, yet on April 24, he informed the government that there was no sign of disturbance. Two days later, he wrote to the king: "All the information

I received on my return [from Versailles] convinces me that complete calm has prevailed all day in the different districts of Paris, particularly in the Faubourg Saint Antoine."

Ironically, major rioting burst out that very day, and persisted until April 28. Different causes have been attributed to it: ferment stirred up by the guilds because Réveillon was so competitive; disgruntled workers — mostly tanners — from the Faubourg Saint Marcel who incited the people; and terrorists and the unemployed.

Of those arrested, some were Réveillon's workmen, but there were others — including the jobless — from various districts. Moreover, in addition to workmen, there were employers as well.

On the night of April 26, unrest had simmered in the cobbled streets of the Faubourg Saint Marcel. Threats were uttered freely against Henriot and Réveillon. The workers, the employers had said, should live on fifteen sous a day, and the citizens would not easily forget their remarks.

On the next afternoon, smoldering hatred burst into action. The insurgents moved off noisily toward the Seine, shouting, "death to the rich, death to the hoarders," and urged that the priests be thrown into the river. At their head they carried figures symbolizing Réveillon and Henriot, and a placard which read: "By order of the Third Estate, Réveillon and Henriot are condemned to be hanged and burnt in the public square."

It looked as if they were going to the palace of the archbishop of Paris. There the general assemblies of the clergy and the Third Estate were in session. The terrified clergy, in fear of their lives, offered to give up their privileges at once. The Third Estate treated the situation more coolly. In the Place Maubert, three of their members tried to calm the rabble and pleaded with it to disperse.

Accounts vary as to what happened next, but later the effigies of Réveillon and Henriot were set alight in the Place de Grève. Still not satisfied, the mob, yelling and cursing, carried on to the Faubourg Saint Antoine.

The way to Titonville barred by fifty grenadiers of the French Guards, the crowd turned in fury on Henriot's home, robbing and damaging it, then burning the furniture and clothing in the Beauvais marketplace. In panic, Henriot escaped by dressing as a servant and seeking sanctuary in the citadel of Vincennes. His family was able to take refuge with friends.

When more troops were called out, the mob scattered. But the next morning thousands again infested the streets in the Faubourg Saint Antoine. Their intention was obvious.

On this day the Duc d'Orléans, driving to Vincennes, passed through the Faubourg Saint Antoine. Orléans smiled and waved from his carriage to shouts of "Long live Orléans, our father, the only true friend of the people!" Among the nobles who followed in carriages, one noted with sarcasm: "Orléans has come to review his troops. Now the big show can begin."

Some historians believe that Orléans was the architect of the Réveillon and other riots — even of the attack on the Bastille. True or not, by returning along this congested route after the meeting, the Duchesse d'Orléans, who demanded to be let through, gave the opportunity for which the crowd was waiting. Perhaps the Guards were at fault for temporarily removing the barricades. But as they did, the mob rushed in, overwhelming the troops and invading the factory.

Titonville was utterly ravaged. Parts of the premises were completely smashed. What would not burn was torn off or broken. In two hours the house and factory were reduced to ruin. Luckily, Réveillon and his family were able to flee unharmed.

As other troops dashed to the spot, the crowd fled into houses and scrambled up the roofs. There they hurled down anything they could rip away — tiles, guttering, and chimney pots — and it took several hours of firing before the troops gained control. Many rioters were killed and some were sentenced to death. Others, found hopelessly drunk in Réveillon's cellars, were sent to prison for life.

Fearing the people in the Faubourg Saint Antoine, Réveillon prudently sought asylum in the Bastille before emigrating to England. The last that is known of Henriot is that he escaped to the citadel of Vincennes.

A Revolutionary Step

The Estates-General opened at Versailles on May 5, 1789, one
week after the uproar subsided. From the outset, no effort was spared
to humiliate the Third Estate. The style of dress had been dictated
beforehand, and the simple black coats of the people's deputies were
in sharp contrast to the elegant dress of the nobility and the cere-
monial robes of the clergy. Moreover, the Third Estate had to enter
through a back door and kneel to present the *cahiers*. The others
passed through the main gateway and stood in the royal presence.
In various petty ways the court took pains to remind the people's

Procession of the Estates-General at Versailles

representatives that they were inferior. On the first day, when the 1,200 deputies walked in stately procession to the Church of Saint Louis for high mass, the Third Estate were placed last. However, the sermon preached by de la Fare, bishop of Nancy, who implied that some reforms were overdue, pleased the people's deputies and angered Marie Antoinette.

On the following day, at the opening session in the Salle des Menus Plaisirs, everyone met the king. To the Third Estate, buoyant with expectation, the monarch's speech had a depressing effect. The reforms to which he referred were trifling compared with those requested by the people.

The deputies met again the next day to confirm their credentials. The orders sat apart. The Third Estate insisted that everyone sit together. After all, they stressed, the nation was represented by all three orders. Actually, this was a preliminary step by the Third Estate to force everyone to vote by head. When the other orders refused to comply, the Third Estate — to show that they declined to accept the existence of three bodies — called themselves the Commons, in the manner of the English Parliament.

Stalemate continued for some weeks. Then on June 17, having attracted a small number of the clergy and urged on by the people, the Third Estate proclaimed itself the National Assembly. It was a revolutionary step, and an illegal one. After centuries of feudalism, the Commons was suddenly snatching power. It contended that it was the National Assembly, since it "represented ninety-six percent of the people." Defiantly, it went so far as to declare that if the Assembly were dissolved, taxation, thereafter, would be illegal. The Assembly was indicating that the nobles and the clergy did not have the right to make laws; even the king could no longer reject the Assembly's decisions.

More members of the clergy now offered to unite with the Third Estate if there was no individual voting. Alarmed, La Rochefoucauld-Liancourt, the chairman, strongly opposed their action, and requested the king to intervene.

By now the court regarded the Assembly's behavior as outrageous. It had gone too far. It was time to destroy it.

First, it was announced that the king would make his will known at a royal session on June 23. To prevent the Assembly from

The oath in the tennis court

meeting before then, the Salle des Menus Plaisirs was closed without warning.

Thus, to their amazement, on the morning of June 20, the people's deputies found the hall locked. Their anger rose as, reading a notice on the door, they learned that workmen were ostensibly preparing the rooms for the royal visit.

Some of the deputies wanted to demonstrate at once in the Place d'Armes. The more fiery were prepared to hold a session beneath the king's window. Finally, the more rational idea of Dr. Joseph Guillotin, one of the deputies, prevailed. They would meet at a seventeenth-century indoor tennis court, the Salle du Jeu de Paume, which was close to the palace. There, in a quiet street, a decision was taken which was to influence all of Europe.

For a table, Jean Sylvain Bailly, the chairman, used a door torn from its hinges. Some of the enraged deputies wanted the Assembly to leave for Paris, but Deputy Jean Mounier, to forestall force by the court, pleaded that all should stay and swear to this oath: "The National Assembly, considering that since it has been summoned to settle the constitution of the kingdom, bring about the regeneration of public order and maintain the true principles of the monarchy, nothing can prevent it from continuing its deliberations, in whatever place it may be forced to meet, and that in a word, wherever its members are assembled, there is the National Assembly, decrees that all the members of this Assembly shall instantly take a solemn oath not to separate, but to meet together wherever circumstances may require, until such time as the constitution of the kingdom shall be firmly established on solid foundations, and all the said members and each of them individually will confirm by their signature this unshakeable resolution."

Only Joseph Martin d'Auch, the deputy for Castelnaudary, refused to swear. It was a decree, he said, that the king had not sanctioned. For that reason he could not comply.

The Assembly had decided on a course which it could not change. From now on, government must be by the consent of the governed, a decision which impressed some of the clergy. Two days later, still barred from the Salle des Menus Plaisirs, the Assembly met in the Church of Saint Louis. There, led by an archbishop, 149 members of the clergy joined the representatives of the people.

The next day was full of drama. The monarch, in a rather threatening speech, offered some reforms. But they did not satisfy the pleas and proposals of the *cahiers*. As if to shatter the National Assembly in one stroke, Louis told the gathering: "Not one of your projects, not one of your resolutions can have force of law except by my special consent. I order you to separate immediately and meet again tomorrow morning, each in the chamber set apart for your order, to resume your discussions."

Obediently, the nobles left, but the Third Estate refused. The Marquis de Dreux-Brézé, master of ceremonies, requested them to go. It was a critical moment. In the background stood the royal troops. The hall was intensely silent for some minutes. Then Bailly, his voice full of defiance, declared that the "assembled nation could take no orders."

The Comte de Mirabeau, deputy for Aix, was even more emphatic, asserting that Dreux-Brézé could go and tell his master that they were there at the will of the people. Only bayonets could compel them to leave.

When he received the news, the king weakly observed that if the deputies wished to remain, they could do so. In a sense, he had no alternative: there were not enough troops in Paris or Versailles to enforce his will. For the time being at least, it was a defeat for the monarchy. But only because the Assembly had the unstinted support of the people of France. Both the people of the towns and the countryside seemed ready to oppose privilege — even the throne.

Resistance among the nobles and the last of the clergy was crumbling. When, on June 25, the Duc d'Orléans and forty-six other nobles joined the National Assembly, the king soon advised the remaining nobles and clergy to unite as well.

Intrigue and Propaganda

The Palais Royal was the residence of the Duc d'Orléans. It stood on the western side of a vast garden, and on the other three sides stretched rows of impressive houses. Straight paths, ornamental pools, and flowerbeds divided the garden, and on the southern side rose a magnificent avenue of chestnut trees. The Café de Foy and the Café du Caveau made huge fortunes there.

Initially, the Palais Royal had been the haunt of the city's social elite. But in 1780 the duke's son, Philippe, transformed it into a public meeting place for aristocracy, bourgeoisie, and working class alike.

Now it had become a "trading palace," with a motley of shops, entertainments, literary salons, and clubs. Here journalists and gossipmongers purveyed their news, giving the Palais Royal a reputation as a center for information — and scandal. Here, too, were housed the advanced cultural societies of the day as well as gambling dens — in short, the rendezvous of scholars, crooks, and thieves.

Most important of all, the Palais Royal was the focal point of political intrigue. Arthur Young, an English traveler who visited it a few weeks before the Bastille fell, wrote that the "business going forward at present in the pamphlet shops is incredible. I went to the Palais Royal to see what new things were published, and to procure a catalogue of all. Every hour produces something new. . . . But the coffee-houses in the Palais Royal present yet more singular and astonishing spectacles; they are not only crowded within, but other expectant crowds are at the doors and windows, listening . . . to certain orators, who from chairs or tables harangue each his little audience; the eagerness with which they are heard, and the thunder of applause they receive for every sentiment of more than common hardiness or violence against the present government, cannot easily be imagined. I am all amazement at the ministry permitting such nests and hotbeds of sedition and revolt. . . ."

The spirit of insurrection among the people and the persuasive propaganda now influenced the troops. On June 24 two companies of the French Guards were ordered to load their muskets, but they disobeyed their officers. Four days later, at the Palais Royal, more military companies assured a crowd that they would not oppose an uprising. And when some of the soldiers were arrested and sent to the Abbaye prison, Loustalot, editor of the *Révolutions de Paris,* incited a mob to set them free. Hussars and dragoons galloped to prevent them, but instead, sheathing their sabers, they fraternized with the crowd.

As a regiment, the French Guards were now in league with the people. And when other soldiers marched into the capital, many hurried to the Palais Royal where they were welcomed by the jubilant throng. So determined were Parisians to foil the court that on July 2, according to a bookseller named Hardy, "a rioting multitude was on the point of setting out from the Palais Royal to rescue the deputies of the Third Estate, who, it was said, were exposed to the danger of being assassinated by the nobles." But the only serious commotion at Versailles occurred on the sixth, when hussars retreated in a tussle with French Guards.

In Paris, even some of the foreign troops succumbed to the orator and the pamphleteer, and showed "strong symptoms of being entirely with the people." Some actually deserted.

Despite the weakening of his forces, the king, spurred on by the queen and her circle, now decided on another unwise act. He agreed to oust his controller-general of finance. Marie Antoinette and the princes had allowed their hatred of Necker to impair their judgment. It is said that in a ridiculous outburst, the Comte d'Artois had even shaken his fist as Necker walked into the ministers' chamber. On July 11, while at dinner, Necker received a letter from the king. It was terse and brutally blunt, ordering him into exile in Switzerland that evening. Necker calmly promised to comply. He would go secretly, and he would depart "alone, without going through Paris, without saying a word to any member of his family." He left immediately, but traveled to Brussels.

On hearing of Necker's dismissal, some of the people's deputies at Versailles hurriedly left their homes, fearing that they would shortly be arrested. In fact, it was the king who was bringing about his own self-destruction. The dismissal was bound to inflame the people, for Necker was their hero and had won their confidence and trust. He had kept the grain hoarders in check, and, in September, 1788, he had suspended the exporting of grain. Moreover, he had safeguarded imports to some extent by giving bounties to those who brought wheat into France. Indeed, seventy million livres had been expended in buying foreign wheat. And as recently as April 23, 1789, he had allowed judges and police officials to make inventories of grain in private granaries.

The Baron de Breteuil, who succeeded Necker, has been described as a man with a loud voice that suggested energy, but his self-confident manners merely deceived those who had faith in their own wishes. In short, Breteuil, lacking money and the guaranteed loyalty of the troops, had no plan. This in itself made possible the coming insurrection in Paris, for a swift and ruthless attack by loyal troops could have broken all resistance.

Desmoulins Incites Revolt

Necker left in the evening. By about nine the next moring the news was widespread at the Palais Royal. Being Sunday, thousands flocked there, avid for news. In fact, the trees bent "under the weight of the people perched on them." Shouting invectives and insults at the court, agitators were soon haranguing the crowds.

On that momentous day, one of the speakers, a shabby young barrister from Guise, would achieve immortality. His name was Camille Desmoulins. Lacking a legal practice, he lived in cheap hotels, depending on a meager income from copying legal documents and other such work. He was emotional and undisciplined, and a passionate disciple of the new political doctrines. Although he lacked judgment and restraint, he was richly endowed with revolutionary fire.

Perhaps his revolutionary fire was all the greater because the citizens of Guise had rejected him as a deputy of the Third Estate. To him it was irksome that a former fellow pupil of the College of Louis-le-Grand, Maximilien Robespierre — whose talents Desmoulins regarded as less than his own — had been chosen. Robespierre would become the leader in the eventual revolution.

Poverty and failure perhaps also warped Desmoulins's outlook, which resulted in extreme views. He thought and spoke passionately in terms of a republic, and on that July day, at about three o'clock, it was Desmoulins who roused the mob. The accounts

Camille Desmoulins

conflict as to what actually happened. In Desmoulins's own version, coming out of the Café de Foy, he mounted a table and cried: "Citizens, you know that the nation had asked that Necker be retained and he has been driven out. Can you be more insolently defied? After such an act they will dare anything. They may perhaps be planning and preparing a . . . massacre on patriots for this very night. To arms! To arms! Let us all wear green cockades, the color of hope. . . ." Then, gesturing to the crowd, he cried: "At least they will not take me alive, and I am ready to die a glorious death! Only one misfortune could befall me — that of seeing France in bondage."

A witness later wrote that Desmoulins merely appealed to arms. In any event, history credits him as the man who incited the Paris uprising. His cry echoed quickly through the *faubourgs*. The theaters, presenting their normal Sunday performances, were hurriedly closed by maddened groups. There could be no entertainment, they cried, when the capital was so seriously threatened.

One group seized the busts of Necker and Orléans from the waxworks show of a man named Curtius. Veiling the effigies in black crepe, they carried them at the head of a vast procession.

In the Place Venture, the demonstrators clashed with dragoons, commanded by the hated Prince de Lambesc, who were rescued by the Royal Allemand regiment. At the Tuileries the cavalry was so pelted with stones from a building site that de Lambesc ordered his men to withdraw. The Marquis de Besenval, commander of troops in Paris, sent reinforcements. But the disturbances went on. And when French Guards, hurrying from their barracks, clashed with a detachment of the Royal Allemand, the latter beat a hasty retreat. Finally, Besenval's troops returned to their camps across the River Seine about midnight.

By failing to suppress the rebels, the insurrection had begun. But the demonstrators were in need of arms. During the night they plundered armorers' workshops, yet this was not enough — certainly not when the king's forces were expected to march on Paris.

Thus, in the *faubourgs* began the hectic task of forging pikes. And throughout the city rang the tocsin, sounding like a note of doom.

On this night the mob set fire to the customs posts, continuing the destruction the next day. That, they thought, would reduce the price of bread. But where, at the moment, was bread to be found?

Ever since June, when the police had carried off nine hundred *setiers* of grain, it had been widely believed that the monastery of Saint Lazare had grain enough for some years. True or not, foodstuffs, thought the rioters, must be plentiful there, for the monastery was also a prison for some five hundred youths. During the morning they ransacked the monastery, loading fifty-three carts with

Above, Desmoulins inciting the mob to revolt. Left, royal troops firing on the people carrying the effigies of Orléans and Necker. Below, the ransacking of Saint Lazare.

flour, and then selling it at the Halles. Silver and books were also seized, and furniture broken. All the prisoners were released.

Now came a cry to liberate more prisoners. The mob rushed to La Force, where debtors were kept, and set free the inmates. Then they demonstrated before other jails. Anarchy reigned in the streets of Paris, to the alarm of the bourgeoisie, who now sought prompt action to suppress the terror.

The Clamor for Arms

Since June 27 the electors of Paris — the people who had chosen the city's deputies for the Estates-General — had, with the agreement of the town council, continued to meet at the Town Hall. On July 12, the electors took the initiative: they appointed a permanent committee to act for the electors as a whole, and then hurriedly formed a citizens' militia. Jacques de Flesselles, the senior city magistrate under the old régime, was chosen as chairman. As for the militia, each of the capital's sixty districts, or bodies of electors, was to raise two hundred men. This figure was soon raised to eight hundred. Only recognized citizens, which in effect meant electors, were to be enrolled.

In this way, the middle class, now fearing the unruly mob, hoped to restore order in the riot-torn city. To recognize each other, the militia first wore a green cockade (a knot of ribbons), but when it was realized that green was the color of the detested Comte d'Artois, they chose the colors of Paris — red and blue.

For the moment, however, muskets were much more vital than cockades, for the terror was getting worse. The task was to find arms.

During July 13, crowds gathered at the Town Hall, clamoring for arms. In the mob were two extremes: those who wanted anarchy and those eager to restore order. De Flesselles was in a quandary, for he did not wish to arm brigands. In fact, judged by his subsequent behavior it seems that he did not wish to arm anyone. It is highly probable that he was communicating with the court.

Initially, therefore, he was evasive, promising the crowd that he would send for arms. But as time went by and the people grew more insistent, he gave way, handing over the few hundred muskets in the Town Hall.

Because these were not enough, artillery was sent for from a factory at Charleville. But when the cases were opened, they contained nothing but rags.

By now the angry mob suspected de Flesselles of deceiving them — more so after he had said that firearms were available at the Carthusian monastery near the Luxembourg. He signed the order instructing the prior to release them, but again the crowd could find no arms.

Next, an appeal was made to Sombreuil, governor of the Invalides complex. But he said that he must first seek permission from Besenval and the authorities in Versailles. Meanwhile, thirty-five barrels of powder, en route for Rouen, were seized at the Port Saint Nicolas and taken to the Place de Grève. There, throughout the night of the 13th, the Abbé Lefèvre d'Ormesson handed out powder to anyone with guns.

Seizing arms and munitions at the Invalides

When no authorization arrived, about 6:00 A.M. on the 14th, thousands impatiently demanded arms. When Sombreuil opened the gates of the Invalides to address them, the mob went wild and rushed in. Some insurgents had already crossed the moat and mounted the parapet, presenting easy targets. But the pensioners, matches in hand, made no attempt to fire the guns, being sympathetic toward the people.

The mob seized twelve pieces of cannon and one mortar and swarmed into the cellars to take more than thirty thousand muskets.

Describing the scene, J. B. Humbert, a watchmaker, wrote: ". . . the crowd at the top of the stairs was so great that all those who were climbing up were pushed down again, and fell right down into the cellar. . . . In spite of this horrible tumble, the crowd persisted in going down the stairs, and as nobody could get up again, there was such a crush in the cellar that people were shrieking and gasping for breath.

"Many people had fainted; so all those in the cellar who were armed followed the advice someone gave and forced the unarmed crowd to turn and go back, threatening them with the points of their bayonets. The advice succeeded, and as the crowd drew back in terror we took advantage of this moment to form a line and force the people up the stairs."

The royal troops were camped nearby, but Besenval, the Paris commander, dared not use them, for he could not count on their loyalty.

Thomas Jefferson, then the United States Ambassador to France, commented later: "It was remarkable that not only the Invalides themselves made no opposition, but that a body of 5,000 foreign troops, encamped within 400 yards, never stirred."

Symbol of Despotism

While the Invalides barracks was being stripped of its arms, another mob was venting its fury on the Bastille. To Parisians nothing symbolized despotism so much as this gloomy fortress-prison built by Charles V in 1370. Its reputation was evil and mysterious, doubtless arising from the secrecy concerning the prisoners. All that was needed to be confined there was a royal warrant. Prisoners arrived in a coach with drawn blinds and, characteristically, the guards were ordered to face the walls. Of all its prisoners, perhaps none had created such an air of mystery and intrigue as that seventeenth-century figure known as "the man in the iron mask."

Many stories grew up about the mysterious prisoner held in the Bastille from 1698 to 1703. He was actually brought to the prison concealed in a mask of black velvet, not iron. The French royal family never revealed his identity. Some say he was Comte Ercole Antonio Mattioli, a minister of the duke of Mantua, and accused of being a spy. Others say he was Eustache Dauger de Cavoye, imprisoned for some unknown offense against the king. But the more romantic explanation, and one used in plays and stories, is that the man in the "iron" mask was the twin brother of Louis XIV. This version says that the prisoner was held in the Bastille to hide his existence from the public, thus ensuring that there would be no dispute over the French throne.

In the public mind, in the Bastille, at the end of the Rue Saint

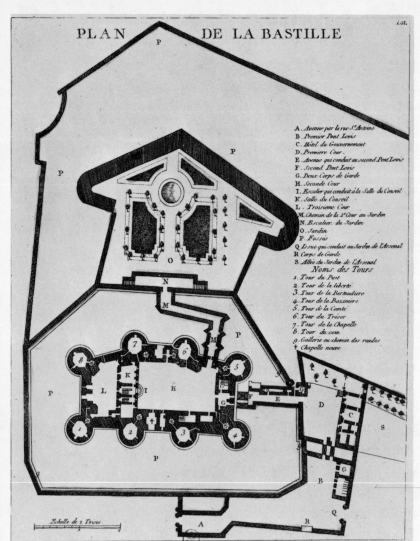

Plan of the Bastille

Antoine, all was "mystery, trick, artifice, snare, and treachery." There were stories of men rotting away behind thick doors with massive locks; of subterranean dungeons — "the resort of toads, of lizards, of monstrous rats and spiders." But the worst story of all concerned the *chambre des oubliettes,* a room of scented flowers and candlelight, where a prisoner, brought before the sadistic governor, would be promised his liberty. Then, at a given signal, the floor would open and the captive would hurl down on to a wheel of knives and be slashed to pieces.

Contrary to what the people thought, under Louis XVI imprisonment in the Bastille had become more humane. The damp dungeons were no longer used. Torture had gradually ceased, and prisoners were not kept in chains. But on July 14, 1789, the howling mob was in no mood to reason. They saw that the cannon were directed menacingly through the embrasures at the streets of the Faubourg Saint Antoine. That roused such anxiety among the people that representatives protested at the Town Hall. The Permanent Committee, therefore, sent delegates to parley with the elderly governor, the Marquis de Launay, who invited them to stay to lunch.

Assured that the Bastille would not be attacked, de Launay withdrew his cannon and had the embrasures blocked with wood.

Apparently de Launay was an indecisive man, and the recent disturbances had so terrified him "that at night he mistook the shadows of trees and other objects round him for enemies." The garrison had little meat and bread, and its strength comprised eighty-two pensioners and thirty-two Swiss Guards.

In those circumstances the governor was only too willing to compromise. But how was he to disperse the mob? For by now the people swarmed in the outer court, not far from the governor's house. Only a moat separated the fortress from the crowd, which, on seeing the cannon removed, wrongly concluded that they were about to be loaded. The deputation, moreover, had so far failed to return and the people feared they were held hostage.

An advocate, Thuriot de la Rozière, and two others, representing the neighboring district of Saint Louis de la Culture, now sought admission to the governor's house. They asked de Launay to let the

Cannon taken from the Invalides were used against the Bastille's garrison.

militia assist in guarding the fortress. But the governor declined, promising that there would be no firing unless attacked. Rozière next pleaded with the garrison to give in, but, although the pensioners had no wish to fire on the people, Lieutenant Deflue, who commanded the Swiss, protested that it would be dishonorable to yield without fighting. For by now there was a serious threat from the mob.

At first the people had marched on the Bastille merely to secure arms and ammunition. But now a seething mass demanded: "We want the Bastille! Down with the bridges!"

To get into the Bastille it was necessary to pass two courtyards bordered by outbuildings. The first was called the Cour du Passage, or Cour des Casernes (the barracks), and was entered by the triple gate of Saint Antoine. On the fortress side of this courtyard stood shops rented out by the governor. At the end of the Cour du Passage a doorway opened on to the Cour du Gouvernement. Facing the doorway lay a moat, crossed by a pair of drawbridges — one used by carriages, the other by pedestrians. Beyond rose the governor's house and the chief armory, then an avenue leading to the main moat and drawbridges at the entrance to the citadel itself.

The Bridges Fall

The crowd was now uncontrollable. Two men, Denain and Davanne, climbed to the roof of a perfumer's shop, then went along the rampart walk into the Cour du Gouvernement. Others came after them. Finding hatchets in the guardhouse, they smashed the chains of the drawbridges, ignoring the shouts of the garrison to withdraw. Both bridges fell and the mob surged over.

At once there burst a volley of shots. No one knew who began the firing, but it would cost de Launay his life. Immediately, there were angry cries of "Treachery!" Many people — certainly those at the rear — thought that de Launay had deliberately let down the bridges to trap them.

Ironically, at the time of the firing of both muskets and cannon, a proclamation, explaining that the garrison would not fire unless attacked, was about to be made in the Place de Grève. But now, as the dead and the wounded began to appear at the Town Hall, stories of de Launay's treachery became more exaggerated.

To try and bring about a cease-fire, the Permanent Committee sent another delegation to the governor. It proved to be futile, for the party, although frantically waving handkerchiefs, was completely ignored. The delegates reported: ". . . they no longer need any deputation; the siege of Bastille, the destruction of the horrible prison, the death of the governor, that is what they clamor for."

A third delegation also failed, and was actually fired on by the garrison. Yet the situation was about to change. While these last delegates were returning to the Town Hall they met French Guards and armed civilians hauling four cannon and a mortar taken that morning from the Invalides. Commanded by an ex-soldier named Pierre Hulin, now manager of the Queen's Laundry at La Briche, they shouted to passersby that they were on their way to the Bastille.

About 3:30 in the afternoon this formidable contingent reached the citadel by way of the Arsenal. Soon they were joined by other armed citizens, led by Second Lieutenant Élie of the Queen's Infantry.

So far the besiegers' efforts had been ragged and lacking in leadership. Now, under Élie and Hulin, the pattern of attack immediately changed. To enable them to advance nearer to the fortress, the infuriated crowd had created a smoke screen by burning carts of manure and straw in the Cour du Gouvernement. Since this now obstructed the cannon, Élie and others, all the while exposed to fire, dragged the blazing carts away, but unfortunately lost two of their number. There was also danger from paving stones and pieces of iron, which de Launay helped to hurl down.

With Hulin's cannon pointing at the citadel's gates, the garrison was divided. The pensioners, who had no wish to fire on fellow citizens, pleaded with the governor to capitulate, but the Swiss urged him to resist the siege.

In the end de Launay said he would capitulate, but only if the garrison went unscathed. The mob, however, would not listen, shouting, "Down with the bridges!"

The Bastille had fifteen cannon, but perhaps it was because of de Launay's humanity that, during the whole siege, only one was

Maillard taking the note pushed through a slit in the Bastille gate

fired. Instead, at about five o'clock a white flag appeared on the Bassinière tower. A hand was seen holding a note in a slit in the Bastille gate.

Accounts differ as to who crossed a plank to get it. Some say it was Élie, but it is generally claimed to be Stanislas Maillard, the son of an usher at a prison. In the note, de Launay threatened to "blow up the garrison and the whole neighborhood unless you accept our capitulation." Yells of "No capitulation!" greeted it, but Élie shouted that, on the word of an officer, no one would be harmed. Thus assured, the governor had the gate to the smaller drawbridge opened. The Bastille had fallen.

*The angry mob dragging de Launay to the
Town Hall*

It has been claimed that de Launay let down the bridge merely
to receive the leaders of the crowd — Élie, Hulin, Maillard, Tour-
nay, Réole, Arné, and Humbert. But soon after they were admitted,
someone lowered the larger bridge.

At once the mob, armed with forks and hatchets, poured in,
but was immediately fired upon. This only increased the invaders'
fury. They roughly disarmed the Swiss and the pensioners, then
took them prisoner. Only du Puget, the governor's assistant, got
away. He turned his coat inside out and deceived the mob.

De Launay was seized by Maillard and Arné, and the rebels
wanted to kill him immediately. Arné, Hulin, and Élie did their best

to protect him. Indeed, in defending de Launay, Hulin himself was injured. Several times the mob snatched the governor away, and each time Hulin, his clothes torn and his face bleeding, hauled him back again. But as the governor was dragged to the Town Hall, the mob, shouting "Hang him!" almost killed him in the fray.

On the Town Hall steps someone thrust a bayonet into de Launay. Others stabbed him until death spared him further torture. The mob now clamored for his head, and Desnot, an unemployed cook, cut it off with a knife and bore it away. Officers on de Launay's staff and three pensioners were also murdered.

De Flesselles was destined to die, too. For failing to supply the necessary arms, he was accused of betraying the people. Some

De Flesselles is murdered.

wanted to imprison him, but finally it was agreed to let him speak at the Palais Royal in his own defense. Yet, as he was leaving the Town Hall, a young man suddenly emerged from the crowd and shot him. De Flesselles's head was also severed and, with de Launay's, was borne to the gardens of the Palais Royal. The Bastille keys were carried on ahead.

That same evening the king, unaware of the turmoil in his capital, and rather tired after the hunt, returned to the palace at Versailles. No deer had been killed that day, so in his diary he wrote one word: "Rien" ("nothing").

Feudal Power Ends

Unfortunately, Louis now listened to the queen and her coterie once again. Had he agreed to accept a constitutional monarchy, he would most probably have been saved. Instead, he summoned his troops to Paris. On July 8 the Assembly petitioned him to withdraw his forces, and the outspoken Mirabeau vehemently condemned the "warlike preparations of the Court."

Louis visited Paris three days after the Bastille fell. Many in the crowd cried "Long live the King!" Bailly, now the mayor, received him, saying: "I bring Your Majesty the keys of his good city of Paris. They are the very ones which were presented to Henri IV; but he reconquered his people, and here the people have reconquered their King. . . ." Bailly later explained that he used the word "reconquered" as a term of affection.

At the Town Hall the people shouted, "Our King, our father," and Louis stuck a red, white, and blue cockade — now the emblem of Paris — in his hat. It seemed that at last there was a firm bond between sovereign and people.

The Bastille itself was to be demolished. Sinister though it was in the minds of the people, when the besiegers rushed to set the prisoners free, to their astonishment they found no more than seven. Four were forgers, one was there at his family's request, and two were insane.

The storming of the Bastille was certainly not a victory in the

military sense. But it did become a symbol of the end of the French monarchy. It came to mark the triumph of a national insurrection over the power of the crown. Through all the events leading up to and ending with the storming of the Bastille, a democratic principle had been established. But it would not have succeeded if the very real economic difficulties of France, which the government proved powerless to correct, had not been present.

The French Revolution was now truly under way. The Paris uprising was soon imitated in many towns and villages of France. Revolutionary town councils and citizens' militias — now called the National Guard — were formed. The peasants attacked the lords' chateaux and burned the old charters concerning seignorial rights.

The climax occurred on the night of August 4 when the National Assembly abolished feudalism by law throughout the country. Three weeks later—on August 26—it announced the Declaration of the Rights of Man and of the Citizen. It proclaimed freedom, equality, the inviolability of property, and resistance to oppression.

Once again, Louis XVI proved extraordinarily unwise. With revolution an accomplished fact, he refused to approve the National Assembly's decrees. And once again the people of Paris took to the streets. They marched to Versailles on October 5 and returned with the royal family.

But it was still not too late for Louis, had he had the sense to see it. The National Assembly established not a republic, but a constitutional monarchy. The king and the Assembly would share the

The old symbol is destroyed.

power. Louis was hostile to the plan, and the constitutional monarchy lasted less than a year.

In 1792, in the midst of all the chaos, France foolishly went to war with Austria and Prussia, a war which would continue until 1815 and involve much of Europe. Also in 1792, the royal family was overthrown. Louis had attempted to flee the country, but he was brought back to Paris and tried as a traitor. He and Marie Antoinette were executed the following year.

The French Revolution would continue in various phases until 1814, with the overthrow of Napoleon. The upheavals it caused and the ideas it unleashed had an effect upon all of Europe. For later generations, the Revolution would serve as a model for the idea that revolution itself could be a specific political process and mission.

A Selected Bibliography

The following works have been helpful in the writing of this book:

Godechot, Jacques. *The Taking of the Bastille*. Translated by Jean Stewart. London: Faber and Faber, 1970.

Kropotkin, P. A. *The Great French Revolution, 1789–1793*. Translated by Henry L. Binsse and Gerard Hopkins. London: Bodley Head, 1960.

Lefebvre, Georges. *The French Revolution from its Origins to 1793*. Translated by Elizabeth Moss Evanson. London: Routledge and Kegan Paul, 1962.

Maurois, Andre. *A History of France*. Translated by Henry L. Binsse and Gerard Hopkins. London: Jonathan Cape, 1956.

———.*An Illustrated History of France*. Translated by Henry L. Binsse and Gerard Hopkins. London: Bodley Head, 1960.

Morton, J. B. *The Bastille Falls*. London: Longmans, Green, 1936.

Webster, Nesta H. *The French Revolution*. London: Constable, 1926.

Index

ABOUT THE AUTHOR

As a Fleet Street (London) journalist, Douglas Liversidge participated in expeditions to the Arctic and Antarctic. He has written a number of books for children, including *The First Book of the Arctic, Arctic Exploration, The British Empire and Commonwealth of Nations,* as well as biographies of Peter the Great, Francis of Assisi, Lenin, Stalin, and Ignatius of Loyola, all for Franklin Watts, Inc. He has also written for newspapers and magazines in over forty countries. Mr. Liversidge, who is married and has one daughter, lives in Pinner, Middlesex, England.